Worn Out Pages

An Invitation Back to The Bible

Jeremy Hall

Dedicated to all those who have been my Bible teachers:

From my parents, to Sunday School teachers.

From High School educators to Seminary Professors.

From the Fundamentalist Conservatives to the Woke Liberals.

From those whose positions I can't stand to those whose I seek to emulate and embody.

From those I've called pastor to those who I've followed online.

From the famous writers and speakers to those you've never heard of.

From those who offered carefully planned lessons to those who had no idea what kind of impact they were making when they shared their perspectives with me.

I am indebted to all of you.

Foreword,

For multiple reasons our culture is reeling in chaos and confusion. We long for a clarifying voice that squares coherence with reality. Dr. Jeremy Hall is a voice of this caliber; intelligent, provocative, creative, and encouraging. I have intentionally studied principles of proper and accurate Biblical Interpretation for years when Jeremy made a couple of statements that gave me a radical explanation for looking at the Scriptures in this present age. He stated, "The Bible is not in contradiction with itself, it is in conversation with itself." As a corollary to that he said, "The Bible contains its own counterpoints throughout its internal dialogue." These statements alone demand further exploration (write another book Jeremy).

Dr Hall has a unique facet of his gifting from the Spirit in that he has the passion and the ability of taking one particular concept and seeing it as a thread from Genesis to Revelation to see how it weaves into the whole counsel of God. He has done this in *WORN OUT PAGES,* navigating through issues of justice and how they relate to community, particularly the people of God.

Along with the printed format, you have access to listening to Jeremy's words from which this project originated. Lori Reece deepens your experience through her stimulating artwork. Enjoy it, talk about it, challenge it, and share it.

Mike Rollwagen

Order of Contents

Author's Introduction i

QR Code v

Art: Disorientation 1

Old Testament 3

Art: Justice 33

Art: Community 59

Art: Reconciliation 87

New Testament 89

Art: Restoration 119

Guide to the Artwork, Lori Reece 150

Author Bio 159

Collaborators' Bios 163

Acknowledgements 169

Author's Introduction,

I was a pastor when Covid-19 came on the scene. I will never forget the meeting where we decided that much of the way we ministered would have to change. We moved our services online, switched our Bible studies and prayer meetings to the ZOOM platform, and almost overnight I morphed from being a pastor to being a content creator. We did our best, and I am proud of the way our congregation navigated the hardest days of the pandemic.

During this time I found myself concerned about the ongoing faith development of my congregation, especially the young people who were falling out of the rhythm of congregational life. I had been on TikTok (a social media platform where creators post 60 second videos that anyone can stumble across), for about a year and had amassed a small but noteworthy following including many of the young people from my congregation.

In May of 2020, I was reading the book of Ezekiel when I noticed the many parallels between the life of the prophet and the current climate in which the high school and college students in my congregation found themselves. So I sat down and filmed a quick video about what Ezekiel has to say to the pandemic-stricken world of 2020. I ended the video with a sarcastic reference to a comment left by an antagonistic TikTok user on one of my earlier videos saying "but hey, the Bible is just an old arcane book with nothing to say to us today, completely irrelevant." This facetious line would give a name to the project that emerged from this first video. For the next several months I produced 65 one minute videos covering all 66 books of the protestant Bible under the title "*The Bible is Irrelevant.*"

What is this book?

This book is an invitation. On each page you will encounter a quick poetic invitation to a book of the Bible that attempts to capture the soul of each of the 66 books of the Bible from the vantage point of the disoriented and tumultuous space of early 21st Century USA. Working this angle, five themes seemed to emerge: Disorientation, Justice, Community, Reconciliation, and Restoration.

One of the beautiful and mysterious things about the Bible is that every time you come back to it in honest, humble curiosity, the Holy Spirit can show you something new. If I were to take this project on again in five years, the themes that grip me and the perspectives I take on the books could be completely different. All this to say, I am by no means telling you "the right answer" or the "correct perspective" or the "best/only interpretation" of the Bible, but rather I am sharing with you what I found compelling about the story from where I am sitting in 2020.

The purpose of these videos and this book is to peak your interest, to invite you back to the Bible to see that there is always something new and relevant waiting for us when we allow the Bible to speak: "As the rain and the snow come down from heaven, and do not return to it without watering the earth and making it bud and flourish, so that it yields seed for the sower and bread for the eater, so is my word that goes out from my mouth: It will not return to me empty, but will accomplish what I desire and achieve the purpose for which I sent it."
(Isaiah 55:10-11).

How does this book work?

There are a few ways that one could journey though this book. Each book of the bible receives a one page treatment, based on a 60 second TIKTOK video, these videos have been re-uploaded to youtube and can be viewed by following the links at the end of this introduction. You will also discover art from Lori Reece, an incredibly talented artist from Pensacola, FL, with a gift for bringing scriptural truths into visual mediums with compelling beauty (you can find her work at https://www.lorireece.art/). She has space in this codex as well to explain her contribution. Her art explores multiple dimensions of how the Bible comes to us, as well as containing the story of redemption, and highlighting some of the core themes of the theological world/interpretive framework I am working with as I present each of these books.

I envision this book as sitting on your desk or nightstand next to your Bible. When you decide to start a new book, or if you find yourself lost in a book, *Worn Out Pages* seeks to help bring context and a frame to what you are reading.

I hope that you find these treatments compelling and inviting and that they give fresh life and perspective to these texts which have meant so much to me and millions of others throughout history. Because the Bible is NOT just an old, arcane book with nothing to say to us, it is completely relevant.

Welcome to *Worn Out Pages:*
An Invitation Back To The Bible.

-Jeremy Hall

Follow this link or scan the QR code below with your smartphone to access the youtube playlist of the original video series.

<u>https://tinyurl.com/bdh5xev4</u>

AFRAID BAD CHAOTIC DISFUNCTIONAL EGOTISTICAL FRETFUL
IGNORANT JADED KEEP LOST MINE NO WORRY OPINION PRIDE QUIT
TROUBLE UNABLE VACILLATE WITHHOLD XING YEARNING ZIG
RESS
RY REVOLT SECRETIVE TRAPPED UNWILLING VIOLE T WAR
Q ROARROGANT BROKEN CRUEL DEATH ENRAGE DFLAW ED
IMMORAL JEERING KICKING LUSTY MOURNING NEED Y

שמע ישראל
יהוה אלהינו
יהוה אחד

THE OLD TESTAMENT

Genesis

The book of **GENESIS** is the *first* book in the Bible
And it starts off by reminding us that...

ALL FAMILIES ARE DYSFUNCTIONAL

and that *life in COMMUNITY is hard,* but
God seeks to join us in our communities.

The God of this BIBLE is a God characterized

by **RELATIONSHIP**

by **ACTION**

by **GENEROSITY**

by **MERCY**

and **KINDNESS**

and a God who is *on a* ***MISSION***

The *DREAM* of this God, throughout this book will be and the *whole* Bible will be to

BLESS ALL THE FAMILIES OF THE EARTH

And this God is looking for *PARTICIPANTS...*
people who can be a blessing, to bring about

LOVING, KIND, and JUST COMMUNITIES

EXODUS

In the book of **EXODUS**
GOD HEARS the
CRY OF THE OPPRESSED
AND MOVES HEAVEN AND EARTH
TO RESCUE THEM

Taking an ENTIRE PEOPLE GROUP that has been
ENSLAVED
And lifts them OUT OF THEIR SLAVERY
And spends decades

BUILDING A **RELATIONSHIP** WITH THEM

and *deprogramming them*
teaching them

HOW TO BE HUMAN AGAIN

and through the book
extending an
INVITATION
to the READER
To COME and
To LEARN

HOW TO BE HUMAN

LEVITICUS

The book of **LEVITICUS**
is one that people
frequently *skip over*
frightened by the
rules
rituals
festivals
and ancient sacrifices

BUT at its HEART LEVITICUS is a book about

COMMUNITY
and
ACTIONS
and
How they have **CONSEQUENCES**

This book demands that if you hurt someone

YOU MAKE IT RIGHT

This is a book about *COMMUNITY*

and *JUSTICE*

and ultimately about

RECONCILIATION

With OURSELVES

With OUR FAMILIES

And with REALITY itself

NUMBERS

The book of **NUMBERS** gets a bad rap
and that's probably because of its **name**
I mean, what could be more boring than a book about **numbers**

But it is actually a book about a **JOURNEY**

The people of God find themselves in the
WILDERNESS
not sure of who they are going to *become*
or what they are *going to do*

And in this place

GOD PROVIDES

GOD SHOWS UP

Even with their *GRUMBLINGS*
their *COMPLAINING*
and their *REBELLION*

GOD CONTINUES

to **PROVIDE**

and **LEAD**

and **GUIDE**

__DEUTERONOMY__

DEUTERONOMY is a Sermon
given by **MOSES**
to the YOUNG among the PEOPLE of God

You see, the first generation that God brought out of Egypt
and LIBERATED FROM SLAVERY
They're Dying
and the Young are
WANDERING

WHAT'S THE **STORY** GOING TO LOOK LIKE **NOW**?!
WHAT PART ARE **THEY** GOING TO PLAY

DO THEY **HAVE WHAT IT TAKES** TO BE THE PEOPLE
THAT THEY ARE **CALLED TO BE**
and MOSES says
YES, YES YOU DO
IF YOU

FAITHFULLY

FOLLOW

OBEY

and
WORSHIP GOD

WHAT DOES THAT LOOK LIKE?

It Looks Like
ACTS of SERVICE
LOVE
KINDNESS
and
JUSTICE

*AND THAT YOU CAN **CHOOSE** TO BE THE KIND OF PEOPLE WHO*
MAKE THE WORLD THAT YOU WANT TO LIVE IN

JOSHUA

The book of **JOSHUA** is
VIOLENT

It is about *WAR* and *CONQUEST*

Early in the book it sets forth that the CANAANITES
the people that Joshua and his army are at war with
are the most *morally reprobate* people in the world

Their morals are completely *askew*

They practice **child sacrifice**

They are deserving of **God's Judgment**

And here comes **JOSHUA**
and his Army
the forces of **LIGHT**

But something **strange** start to happen

It starts small with individuals like ***RAHAB***

But a little before midway in the book
Entire Canaanite TOWNS, and PEOPLES
are **joining** the forces of **GOOD**
This book serves to show us that

NO ONE
IS
BEYOND
MERCY
or a
SECOND CHANCE

JUDGES

The book of **JUDGES**
Is a
TRAGEDY

It shows that even the **people of God**
are *VULNERABLE*
to being *TRAPPED in CYCLES*

of *brokenness*

of *violence*

of *injustice*

but that **JUSTICE** and **GOODNESS**
can be **reclaimed**
if we're willing to

Break
Our
Cycles

We **break our cycles** when we
RECOGNIZE
that
WE
have been part of the problem
and
WE
REPENT

which ALWAYS
OPENS UP
A WAY for
RESCUE

RUTH

RUTH
Is a short story
that opens with
TRAGEDY and DEATH
but ends in
JOY and BIRTH

It is the story about the *JOURNEY*
that a *FAMILY* goes on

It is a story about
seemingly **IMPOSSIBLE ODDS**
shocking **COINCIDENCE**
and WOMEN *who work hard
to take control
of their FUTURES*

By the end of the book
we've been led to
ASK QUESTIONS
about how
GOD
was part of THEIR STORY all along
and invites our curiosity
about how

**GOD
MIGHT BE
ACTIVE
IN OUR LIVES**

I SAMUEL

The book of **I SAMUEL**
is the Story of **ISRAEL**
being CONSOLIDATED
from a group of *RELATED TRIBES*
into a
UNIFIED KINGDOM
under King Saul
and then King David

It is also a WARNING against
PRIDE
and
ARROGANCE

The stories of Saul and David are

TRAGEDIES

They are both promising leaders
with everything going for them
but they are
DEEPLY FLAWED
and their
failure to
CONFRONT
their
CHARACTER FLAWS
ULTIMATELY
leads to their
DOWNFALL

II SAMUEL

The book of **II SAMUEL**
is a book about
DISSONANCE

The great King David
who we are told is a
man after God's own heart
is also a *rapist* and a *murderer*

His family is so
dysfunctional
that it basically
cannibalizes
itself
and it leads to
CIVIL WAR

His son King Solomon
we are told is the wisest man who ever lived
But by the end of the book
He's building a Temple
to the GOD who

LIBERATED THEIR ENSLAVED ANCESTORS
with
A SLAVE LABOR FORCE

And we start to see
that the GOD who is always on the side of the
OPPRESSED
is now going to have to
ACT AGAINST
GOD'S OWN PEOPLE
because they have become the
OPPRESSORS

I KINGS

The book of **I KINGS**
starts with a man named
SOLOMON
He's being enthroned as the new ruler of the
JEWISH KINGDOM

We're told he's a *good man*
and a *God-fearing man*
We're even told that he is
the *WISEST MAN*
who ever lived
BUT
He is quickly corrupted

by **greed**

by **power**

and **lust**

And he takes the people from looking at
A *NEW GOLDEN ERA*
to an age

of *confusion*

and *division*

with a *disaster*

on the horizon

By the end of Solomon's rule
he has built a temple to the God
who **Liberates Slaves**
by MEANS of
SLAVE LABOR

The book reminds us to never put all
our HOPE

our FAITH

or our TRUST

in politicians

II KINGS

The book of **II KINGS**
is TRAGIC in its VIOLENCE

The Kingdoms of
ISRAEL in the NORTH
and **JUDAH** in the SOUTH
Spiral out of Control

with *injustice*
and *idolatry*
and *violence*
to the point where
the KINGS
the ones who are supposed to
PROTECT

Justice and Peace

are INSTITUTING

Violence and Oppression

at a systemic level
which leads to
a *CONSTANT CYCLE*
of *oppression*

violence

revolt

revolution

and *disaster*
until things get
so bad
that the *ONLY ANSWER* is
EXILE
and *TOTAL DISASTER*
for the people of
ISRAEL and **JUDAH**

I CHRONICLES

The book of **I CHRONICLES**
is written at a time of
confusion and *uncertainty*
for the people of God

They have come home from *exile*
and *re-establish* themselves in the *promised land*

BUT THINGS ARE NOT HOW THEY THOUGHT THEY WERE GOING TO BE

They **have not** entered
a **NEW GOLDEN AGE**

They **have** entered
an *AGE OF ANXIETY*

The leadership seems to have failed them
and *NOTHING* is going the way *THEY HAD HOPED*

The first word in the book is
the name ADAM

To try to **CHART A WAY FORWARD**
they **LOOKED BACK**

*They revisit the stories of their heroes
and their great leaders
and they ASK QUESTIONS like*
What should a leader be like
and
**What sort of qualities do we want
as people
MOVING INTO THE FUTURE**

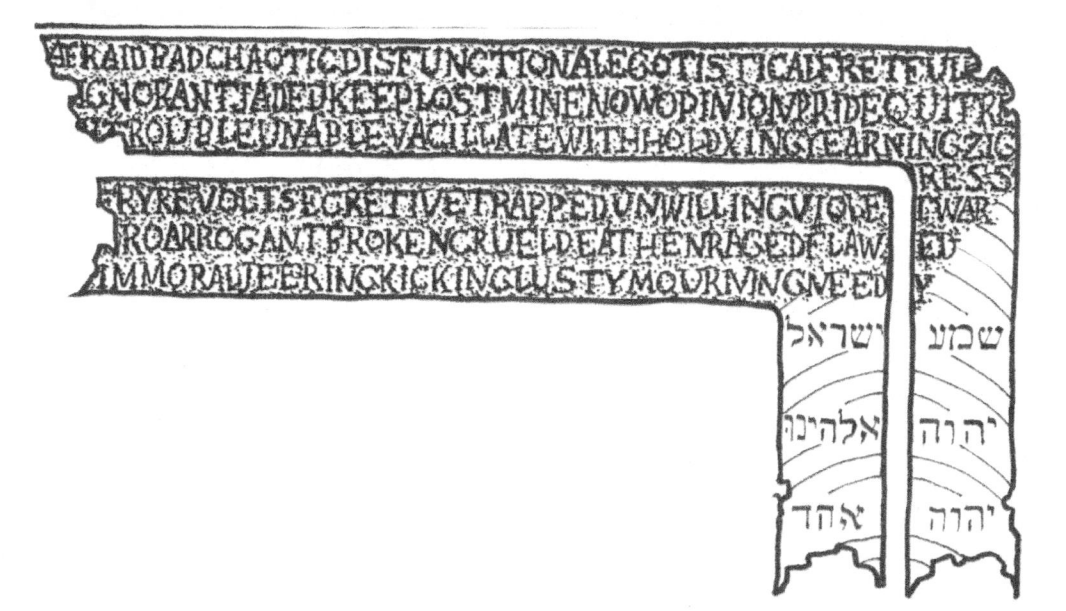

AFRAID BAD CHAOTIC DISFUNCTIONAL EGOTISTICAL FRETFUL IGNORANT JADED KEEP LOST MINE NO OPINION PRIDE QUIT TROUBLED UNABLE VACILLATE WITHHOLDING YEARNING ZIG

RY REVOLT SECRETIVE TRAPPED UNWILLING VIOLE... WAR ...RO ARROGANT BROKEN CRUEL DEATH ENRAGED FLAW... IMMORAL JEERING KICKING LUSTY MOURNING NEED...

שמע ישראל יהוה אלהינו יהוה אחד

JUSTICE

Lori Reece

II CHRONICLES

The book of **II CHRONICLES**
opens in the *MIDDLE* of the story
and ends on an *INCOMPLETE SENTENCE*

The book is a collection
of **character studies**
of the Kings of Jerusalem
after David

and invites us to ASK QUESTIONS
about **loyalty**
and **faithfulness**
and what it means to be a
good leader
and a **good person**

The story
Starts and Stops
in an
Incomplete Place
to remind us that

We're on a *JOURNEY*

that *this* MOMENT
is somewhere
IN THE MIDDLE
and
WE ALWAYS HAVE THE CHANCE
to

CHOOSE
WHAT
COMES
NEXT

EZRA – NEHEMIAH

The books of **EZRA** and **NEHEMIAH**
go together as a single coherent narrative

They are often remembered
as a story of *reconstruction*
but really they are also a story of
failure

The exiled people of JUDAH
returned home
and three leaders are raised up
to set things right
ONE to *REBUILD the TEMPLE*
ONE to *ESTABLISH PROPER WORSHIP*
and ONE to *ESTABLISH CIVIL ORDER*
BUT
In doing so all of them create
an **Insider/Outsider class**
and an **Us vs Them**
and so none of their reforms last

At the end of the books we see
that things are
falling apart
just as soon as they have been *established*
And one of our heroes
arrogantly shouts
At least I tried

It is important that when we
CREATE A NEW WORLD
when we establish

JUSTICE

and ***ORDER***

and ***BEAUTY***

that we
WELCOME EVERYONE INTO IT
Otherwise It cannot LAST

ESTHER

The book of **ESTHER**
is about a *young woman*
who is ***unexpectedly thrust***
into a world of
OVERSIZED EGOS
IDENTITY POLITICS
and SECRET CONSPIRACIES

She discovers that she
HAS A PART TO PLAY IN THE STORY
and that she has
THE OPPORTUNITY TO INTERVENE
on behalf of
JUSTICE

But to do so is
DANGEROUS
It could cost her life

But she steps up and
CHOOSES
to be a
VOICE
for the
VOICELESS

We remember her
for the courageous line
IF I PERISH, I PERISH

40

JOB

The book of **JOB**
Contains one of the oldest stories in the Bible

It is about a man named **JOB**
who we are told is one of the
best men in the world
but then
EVERYTHING
FALLS APART
for Job
And he asks
WHY?

The book invites us to ask

WHY?

His friends come around and offer
all sorts of
philosophical and religious explanations
for what has happened to him

Eventually even the
Voice of God
chimes in to try to bring
CONTEXT to Job's suffering
But none of it answers the question
WHY
this has happened Because sometimes
LIFE IS HARD
and the right thing to do is to ask
WHY
and to be
ANGRY ABOUT IT
and to
FIGHT
for a
BETTER WORLD

PSALMS

The **PSALMS**
are a *COLLECTION*
of *PRAYERS*
and *POETRY*
and *SONGS*
that deal with moments of
ECSTATIC WORSHIP

and the *DEPTHS*
of ***defeat***
and ***fear***
and ***depression***

If we let it the book will teach us
COURAGE
and **MERCY**
and **COMPASSION**

It can give us the
Words
to Articulate
what it means
TO BE HUMAN

It gives us what we need to
NAVIGATE
the
DARK NIGHT OF THE SOUL
and PERMISSION
to FEEL
all of the things
that make us

TRULY HUMAN

PROVERBS

The book of **PROVERBS**
is more than a *collection*
of *wise sayings*
It reminds us that
WISDOM (CHOKMAH in Hebrew)
is an **attribute**
of the **Divine**
And anytime that we use
our
CREATIVITY
to make a
BETTER
and more
BEAUTIFUL
and more
JUST
WORLD
that we are tapping into a
DIVINE REALITY
and
JOINING GOD
In the
RE-CREATION OF ALL THINGS

and more than that
the book encourages us to do it!

It gives us
the *tools*
the *encouragement*
the *courage*
the *motivation*
to become a
PERSON OF WISDOM

ECCLESIASTES

The book of **ECCLESIASTES**
opens with the
Hebrew word *HEVEL*
which can be translated as
smoke or *meaninglessness*

The book can be a bit of a *downer*

It deals with the questions of
Death and *Finitude*
the *Onward Progress of Time*
and
How Things Are Not FAIR

The book asks questions like

Why do people get sick

Why do people have to die

Why do bad things happen to good people

Why do the wicked get ahead

Why does injustice survive in the world

And in asking these hard questions
the book gives us permission
to do the same

SONG OF SONGS

SONG OF SONGS
is a collection of
ANCIENT LOVE POETRY
found in the MIDDLE of the Bible
In a section called
WISDOM LITERATURE

And what is the wisdom of this book?

It is the wisdom of
two young lovers
OBSESSED
with each other
So lost in the
JOY OF THE PURSUIT
that they say that

LOVE is as strong as death
No water can quench it
No ocean will drown it
Its passions are as the grave
You cannot buy it
You cannot sweep it away
You can only be taken by it

And it sits in the MIDDLE of the Bible
to serve as a reminder
that this kind of

LOVE
is a gift from God

And where does the book find its
CLIMAX
In the young woman
finding her agency
in herself

ISAIAH

The book of **Isaiah**
is about a man sent from God
**to confront the powerful ruling systems of the day
to call them out for**

their *injustice*
their *violence*
their *cruelty*
towards the *poor*
the *sick*
the *orphan*
the *widow*
the *foreigner*

And to **warn** them

because of **their actions**
if they do not change
that
DISASTER IS ON THE WAY

But even in the face of this disaster
there is
A MESSAGE OF HOPE

HOPE

Is on the move
even in a broken and troubled world

GOD IS ALIVE
and
GOD IS ON THE MOVE

on behalf
of
JUSTICE

JEREMIAH

The book of **JEREMIAH**
is about a *prophet-priest*
who is called to
warn the people of God
about the CONSEQUENCES
of their
INJUSTICE and ***IDOLATRY***

The book tells us that there are
REAL and SEVERE
CONSEQUENCES
for our actions
and that

GOD IS JUST

And the **JUSTICE of GOD**
will always find its own mark

BUT

That the **LOVE** and **MERCY of GOD**
are even stronger
and that eventually

MERCY *WINS*

and by following God
we can find a way forward
out of the
confusion and *catastrophe*

<u>LAMENTATIONS</u>

The book of **LAMENTATIONS**
is a *collection* of *poems*

The first word of the book
is the Hebrew word ***EKHAH***
meaning **HOW**

This gave the book its original name
The book of **HOW**

HOW did we get here
HOW did this happen
HOW is any of this even possible
These are the questions that the book asks

The book
SITS IN SOLITARY
With anyone who has ever experienced

Injustice

wound

violence

or ***trauma***

and invites us into a place
where we can
recognize those experiences as VALID
where we can
name them as HOLY
and the
victims as SACRED

It invites us into a place of
AUTHENTICITY
in a world that is so often
plastic
and *artificial*
and *superficial*

__EZEKIEL__

The book of **EZEKIEL**
is about a young man
whose life is *torn apart*
when his society collapses around him
because of outside forces
that are *beyond his control*

It is on the day that he is supposed to graduate
that he finds himself

ISOLATED
and
ALONE

somewhere he
NEVER
EXPECTED
TO BE

And it is **HERE**
that
GOD SHOWS UP

NOT in a Temple
NOT in a religious ceremony
but
ALONE
IN ISOLATION
IN
EXILE
is where
EZEKIEL
ENCOUNTERS
The
DIVINE

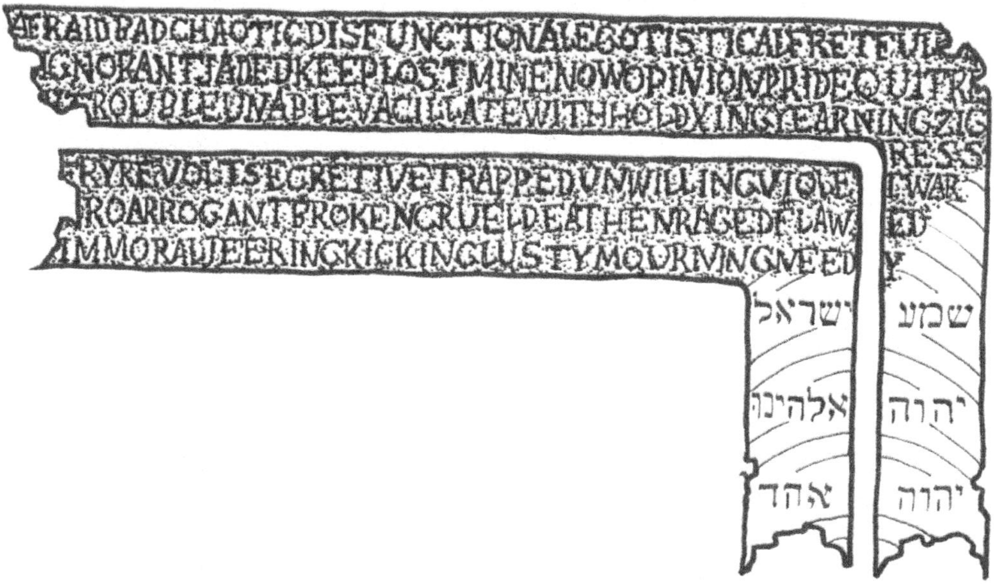
שמע ישראל
יהוה אלהינו
יהוה אחד

JUSTICE
COMMUNITY
κοινωνία
ΙΧΘΥΣ
צדק
משפט
Lori Reece

DANIEL

The book of **DANIEL**
is set during a time of
EXILE

The main characters have been defeated
and carried away as
victims
as the *defeated*
as *prisoners*
as *refugees*

And they are trying to figure out
how to live in a world
completely outside
their EXPERIENCE
or **EXPECTATIONS**

And the answer the book comes up with
Is that you can live
In this sort of world
by a
COMMITMENT
to
principles
and
values
and relying on your
COMMUNITY
and
CREATIVITY

HOSEA

The central message of the book of **HOSEA**
is that
GOD'S LOVE
and
FAITHFULNESS
are
UNQUENCHABLE
even towards those who
DO NOT DESERVE IT

and that you can
ALWAYS
FIND YOUR WAY BACK TO GOD

Hosea himself *reminds* us that
the *way you live*
and *what you do*
is often more important
than **what you believe**
or **what you say**

JOEL

The book of **JOEL**
is about a time
of ***natural disaster***
of ***unprecedented***
and ***unexpected cataclysm***

and Joel ASKS QUESTIONS like

Has anything like this ever happened before?

What does God have to do with this?

Can our economy survive?

What sort of values matter right now?

How could we ever find a way forward?

AMOS

The book of **AMOS**
is about a man

ENRAGED BY INJUSTICE

He is *so disgusted* by what he sees
that he leaves
his HOME
his FARM
his JOB

to *CONFRONT the POWERFUL*
who were
guiding his society

His MESSAGE to them

GET YOUR PRIORITIES STRAIGHT
PEOPLE MATTER
TAKE CARE
of the
poor and disinherited
BRING ABOUT JUSTICE

Let justice roll down like a river
like a stream into dry places

OR

BE

DESTROYED

OBADIAH

The book of **OBADIAH**
is the shortest in the Old Testament

It deals with **questions**
of *war*
and *conflict*
and *conquest*

It deals with **struggles**
between *families*
between *races*
between *nations*

And it identifies all the evil that it sees in

PRIDE

PRIDE is what causes nations
to brutalize each other

PRIDE is what causes people
to mistreat refugees

PRIDE is what causes most
of the world's issues

and
Obadiah points to a day
when
TRUTH
will win out over
PRIDE
and invites us to
STEP INTO
THAT REALITY
NOW

JONAH

The book of **JONAH**
is
NOT
about a
Fish

it is not really even about
JONAH

The book of JONAH is about
the
radical

shocking

exhilarating

terrifying
FACT
that
GOD LOVES MORE PEOPLE
than you do

GOD IS ON A MISSION
to
RECONCILE THE WHOLE WORLD
TO HIMSELF

Even those the *people of God*
consider ENEMIES
are on God's list

for **LOVE** and **PEACE**
and **HOPE** and **RESTORATION**
and *SALVATION*

MICAH

The book of **MICAH**
is a *WARNING*

God sends the prophet Micah
to *WARN*
the leaders of Israel and Judah
that their
INJUSTICE HAS CONSEQUENCES

That God
Wil Not
Allow
OPPRESSION
to
Survive

It is also a CALL
to **SEEK JUSTICE**
to **LOVE MERCY**
to **WALK HUMBLY**
to **LOVE FERVENTLY**
and
to **WAIT PATIENTLY**

Because in the CONTEXT of
the **KINGDOM OF GOD**

JUSTICE IS ALWAYS ON THE MOVE
and
JUSTICE IS ALWAYS ON THE WAY

NAHUM

The book of **NAHUM**
is written to a
defeated and *troubled*
people

The name **NAHUM**
means
COMFORT
and that is what the book is meant to do

The **vision** this prophet has
is of

God's nature
in regards to
JUSTICE

Nahum
reminds us that

GOD CANNOT ENDURE INJUSTICE

and
that God
Is always on the move
on behalf of the
oppressed

and that
ALL
Aggressive
and
Unjust
EMPIRES
eventually
FALL

HABAKKUK

The book of **HABAKKUK**
is a *CONVERSATION*
between the prophet and God

They discuss
corruption
in government and leadership
and Habakkuk asks God

**DO YOU SEE ALL THE EVIL
IN THIS WORLD
ARE YOU EVER GOING TO DO SOMETHING**

And God *RESPONDS* that

God **SEES**
God **LOVES**
and
God is **ALWAYS**
ON THE MOVE
to bring about
JUSTICE
in the world

The book is ultimately an
ENCOURAGEMENT
and a
DISCUSSION
of how
to live
in the
WAITING

ZEPHANIAH

The book of **ZEPHANIAH**
is written by an *insider*

The prophet Zephaniah has *privilege*
He is part of the *religious system*
He is of the *upper class*
of a *high stock*
and he sees the **corruption**
that is taking place
under the guise of
REFORM

He sees that the **system** is
rotten to the core
and he uses his *privilege*
to speak to the *powerful*
and
CALL THEM OUT

He uses **poetry**
that has images of
the world
being
deconstructed
uncreated
to explain how God
is going to respond
to those who
create systems of
INJUSTICE

BUT
THERE IS
HOPE
FOR THOSE
WHO
CHOOSE
A BETTER WAY

HAGGAI

The book of **HAGGAI** is written
when the _EXILES_
the _people of God_
have come back from
BABYLON
to the city of
JERUSALEM
They have a **City**
kind of
They have a **King**
kind of
They have a **Temple**
Kind of
THE FUTURE IS IN QUESTION
We do not know what is going to happen next
BUT
Haggai reminds us of
God's Dream
to bless all of the families
of the world
and invites us
into
PARTICIPATION
of that Dream
He reminds us
that
Our CHOICES
Our PRIORITIES
Our DECISIONS
THEY MATTER
That we might strive to be people
of **JUSTICE**
of **BEAUTY**
of **GOODNESS**
Who deserve to live in
the
NEW CREATED WORLD
And this motivation should motivate us
to **_deep humility_**
and **_decisive action_**

ZECHARIAH

In the book of **ZECHARIAH**
the people of God have come back to
THE LAND
but things **are not** the way
that they **expected them to be**

They thought that they would be entering
a *NEW AGE*
of *blessing* and *prosperity*
BUT THEY HAVEN'T
And they cannot quite figure out why

Zechariah brings up the
state of the Temple in Jerusalem
They have rebuilt the
city and **their homes**
but they have left the

Religious Center

of their world

in

SHAMBLES

And he tells them that if you want
to live in a world
of **JUSTICE**
and **PEACE**
and **LOVE**
and **GOODNESS**
You are going to have to

RECENTER GOD

in your life
and in your society

MALACHI

The book of **MALACHI**
is the last book of the Old Testament

It takes place after the people of God
have returned home to The Land
after the *EXILE*
and they expect a
NEW GOLDEN AGE
to emerge
but it
doesn't

And so
GOD CALLS THEM OUT

saying that you have allowed
corruption to take root
in government
and religion

YOU HAVE FORGOTTEN
the importance of FAMILY

YOU HAVE NEGLECTED
your responsibility for UNITY

YOU HAVE NEGLECTED
your responsibility
to **CREATE** a **JUST SOCIETY**

But
God says that if you are willing to
Start Again
and to
Put in the Work
to
BUILD A BETTER WORLD
I WILL JOIN YOU IN THAT WORK

87

THE NEW TESTAMENT

Matthew

MATTHEW is one of the GOSPELS in the Bible
It tells the STORY of the life of

JESUS of NAZARETH

And this is the most JEWISH of all the Gospels

It wants us to understand that
JESUS is a DIRECT CONTINUATION of
the STORY that the OLD TESTAMENT was telling of

the blessing of the *WHOLE WORLD*

and that JESUS is a *NEW MOSES*

that JESUS is a *NEW KING*

and that JESUS is ***EMMANUEL,***

an old word that means ***GOD WITH US***

This book contains STORIES and MANIFESTOS and TEACHINGS

about **LOVE**

and **COMMUNITY**

and **JUSTICE**

and **GOD**

But most importantly the book shows us that GOD:

ULTIMATE SOURCE
GROUND of BEING

that capital "T" **TRUTH** and capital "L" **LOVE**

has not abandoned us but CARES DEEPLY
about HUMANS and about CREATION

MARK

In the Gospel of **MARK**

GOD SHOWS UP
In *HUMAN FORM*

and in *HUMAN SPACE*
in the Person of

JESUS

Now Mark's JESUS is a *DOER*
JESUS is *GOING PLACES*
He's *DOING THINGS*
He's *HEALING* folks

He's meeting people and He's doing this to *show* us

WHAT GOD IS LIKE

This is a God
Who is **INTERESTED**
Who is **ACTIVE**
Who is **PRESENT**

And part of the central message or Mark's JESUS is that
If you want to be a **LEADER**
you have to learn to be a **SERVANT**

The more leadership you seek to have
the greater your capacity must be to **SERVE**
And **HE** didn't just *SAY* these things,

He **SHOWS UP** And **DOES THEM**

LUKE

The Gospel of **LUKE** seems to be a *reactionary document*

It seems like It was written to **set the record straight** about the Life and Ministry of JESUS of NAZARETH

It seeks **answers to questions** about

FAMILY
and
LOVE

WOMEN
and
FEMININITY

It deals with *issues* of

WEALTH
and
POVERTY

And *questions* of

SIN
and
FORGIVENESS
and of
FATE
and
FREEWILL

JOHN

The Gospel of **JOHN** is *COSMIC*

The author starts with JESUS
BUT QUICKLY ZOOMS OUT
TO SHOW US THE FULL STREAM OF
DEEP TIME IN THE COSMOS
THEN BRINGS US BACK
to a MAN In Nazareth
with the

FULL EXTENT
of the
VERY NATURE
And
POWER OF GOD
CENTERED IN
ONE PERSON

JESUS is **POWERFUL** and **MYSTERIOUS**

But *AT THE SAME TIME*
this **JESUS** is *COMPASSIONATE*
LOVING
CLOSE
and
PERSONAL

THE
PERFECT COMBINATION of
TOTALLY GOD
and
TOTALLY MAN
SENT TO EARTH ON A
MISSION OF LOVE

To show us what it would be like to
Live in a World Made **WHOLE**

ACTS

The book of **ACTS**
is the **STORY** of the **SPREAD**

the SPREAD of the CHURCH

It starts with **JESUS** telling His **FIRST FOLLOWERS** to spread the MESSAGE

of *LOVE*
of *RECONCILIATION*
of a *GOD*

WHO CARES ABOUT PEOPLE
and to
TAKE THAT MESSAGE TO THE WHOLE WORLD

Acts SHOWS us HOW that HAPPENS
And as we do the **HOLY SPIRIT** LEADS
those **FIRST FOLLOWERS** into

STRANGE
and
UNEXPECTED
PLACES
Forcing them to
INTERACT WITH PEOPLE THEY WERE TAUGHT TO
HATE
And
THEY TURN THE WORLD UPSIDE DOWN
through

HOSPITALITY
LOVE
and
RADICAL WELCOME

<u>ROMANS</u>

The book of **ROMANS**
*RECOGNIZES that there is something
TERRIBLY WRONG with the WORLD*

that something fundamental is

BROKEN DEEP DOWN

in what it means to be a created thing

The author calls it **SIN**
it's **DEATH**
it's **INJUSTICE**
it's the **BROKENNESS**
that we LIVE WITH

BUT THERE IS AN ANSWER

BECAUSE the GOD of the BIBLE

DOES NOT ABANDON PEOPLE
to sin and death
BUT RATHER **MAKES A WAY** TO ESTABLISH A

NEW HUMANITY

IN A *NEW CREATION*

And ALL of it is a
GIFT
that can be RECEIVED
and a
GIFT
that can be
SHARED

I CORINTHIANS

I CORINTHIANS
reminds us that we get to
CHOOSE
Who We Are
and How We Live

Paul writes this letter to a church that he planted in Corinth
because they have *STRUGGLES*
The Christians in Corinth
are *NOT DOING WELL*

The Church is *DIVIDED* and full of *CONFLICT* over things like

FOOD
and SEX
and ETHICS
and WORSHIP
and THEOLOGY

And Paul points out that all of their struggles are coming from the
FACT that they are NOT
LIVING in LINE
WITH WHAT THEY SAY THEY BELIEVE

Wen our lives get out of whack
with our **VIRTUES**
and our **PRINCIPLES**
WE GET OURSELVES INTO ALL SORTS OF TROUBLE
But the **GOOD NEWS** here is that we get to
CHOOSE
WHO WE ARE and
HOW WE LIVE

This book CHALLENGES US to
CHOOSE
HIGHER THINGS
and to find
FREEDOM IN IT

II CORINTHIANS

The book of **II CORINTHIANS**
addresses many topics

It talks about
Reconciling Broken Friendships
It deals with
How to Live in Community
And it deals with
How to Credential Leaders
The author Paul says that when thinking about
LEADERSHIP

You shouldn't judge people based on their
STATUS
or *WEALTH*
or *ELOQUENCE*
but rather the **true tell of a leader**

is in the
WAY THEY LIVE

It's in the
PRODUCT THEY PRODUCE
in
INDIVIDUALS
and
COMMUNITIES

It's about the way that they
LIVE THEIR LIFE

in the way that they actually
TREAT PEOPLE

GALATIANS

The book of **GALATIANS**
is written by a man named PAUL
to a community in a time of *trouble*
The church in the city of Galatia has become

Fractured Split and *Conflicted*

along the lines of
Practice and *Conduct*
and most importantly *RACE*

And Paul is **SHOCKED**
Because this has

NO PLACE
In the Kingdom of God
NO CONTEXT
In the teachings of the Bible
or of JESUS

And so he tells them that they need to
REFRAME
their whole community
understanding that they are part of a

NEW KIND OF PEOPLE
A NEW WAY OF BEING HUMAN

that is centered around HIGHER REALITIES like

LOVE
JOY
PEACE
PATIENCE
and
KINDNESS

EPHESIANS

The book of **EPHESIANS**
DIVES into some DEEP topics
like the

MYSTERY of GOD'S ACTIVITY in HUMAN HISTORY
both *PHYSICAL*
and *SPIRITUAL*

It asks QUESTIONS about
the *NATURE of GOD*
and the *NATURE of COMMUNITY*
and invites us to

JOIN GOD
In **GOD'S DREAM**
to **bless all the families of the earth**

and tells us that when we join God on
this **MISSION** this **QUEST**
We discover an entirely

NEW WAY of BEING HUMAN

that changes the way that we relate to

the **DIVINE**

to the **NATURAL**

to **OURSELVES**

and to our **COMMUNITIES**
that make us all part of

ONE FAMILY
MADE NEW

PHILIPPIANS

PHILIPPIANS
is written by a man named PAUL
and he writes this book as a letter to his friends
while *sitting in prison*
most likely *awaiting his* **execution**
And in **this time**
this **place**
HE CHOOSES
to write about

JOY

He says that it is connected

to *COMMUNITY*

to *SERVICE*

to *PURPOSE*

and that **JOY** is a

CHOICE

regardless of **CIRCUMSTANCES**

We can

CHOOSE JOY

as our

CENTRAL REALTY

taking us out of the struggles of the moment
and allowing us to **LIVE** in the **context**

of the

GRAND STORY

of the

RECONCILIATION

of

ALL CREATION

COLOSSIANS

COLOSSIANS
Reminds us
that we have a CHOICE
in the WAY WE LIVE OUR LIVES

We even have a CHOICE
in the KIND of WORLD
we're going to LIVE IN

We *CREATE the WORLD*
by *LIVING in it*

If we **SEEK a COMMUNITY**
of **JUSTICE**
and **RIGHTEOUSNESS**
of **PEACE**
and of **LOVE**

We have to
BUILD
that
COMMUNITY

And in doing so we'll find ourselves

MEMBERS
of a
NEW FAMILY
Bigger than any social construct

I THESSALONIANS

I THESSALONIANS
Is a letter written by one of the earliest Christians
to a community in Thessalonica

This community is experiencing
Extreme Persecution
Danger
and Threats to Their Very Existence

Paul tells them that
If they are going to survive
It is going to be because of

their FAITH
their HOPE
and in their LOVE

for each other
for God
and for their community

They are going to **WIN**
not by resisting what they hate
but by
CHOOSING to be PASSIONATE about something
to be
PEOPLE of LOVE

119

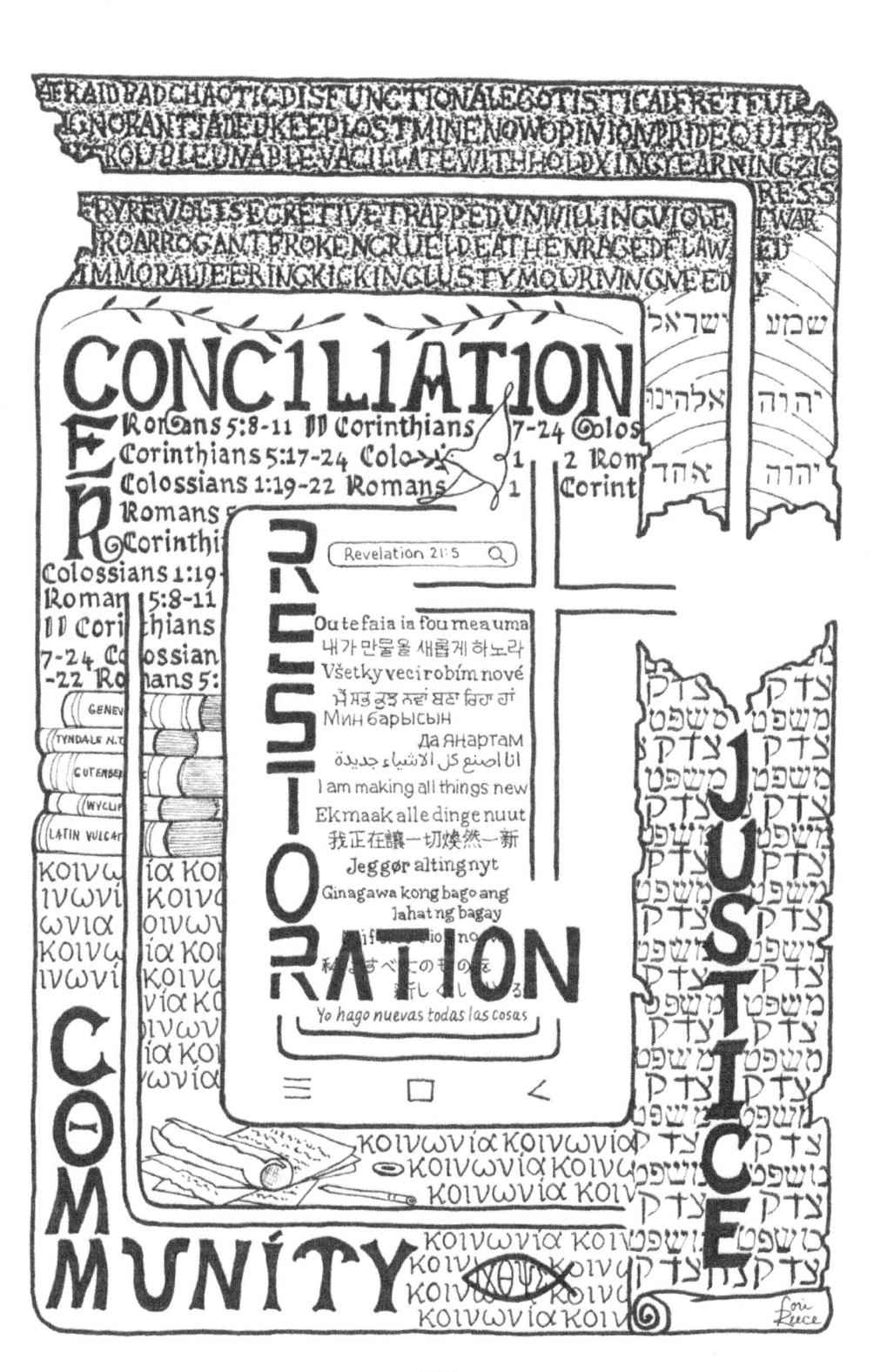

II THESSALONIANS

The book of **II THESSALONIANS**
reminds us that
the *NEW WORLD*
is not going to
BRING itself into BEING

but that the work of

JUSTICE

Is often fraught with

CONFLICT
TROUBLE
and PAIN

But that through
COMMUNITY and **CONNECTION**

with *Love for each other*
for *those we serve*
and for *GOD*

That we will find **PEACE** in the work
and ultimately this work
CONNECTS us with the ground of ALL BEING

and the
PROMISE
of **JUSTICE**
and **PEACE**
and a
BETTER WORLD

I TIMOTHY

The book of **I TIMOTHY**
is a letter from Paul
to his young protégé TIMOTHY

Timothy has been sent to Ephesus
to *CONFRONT CORRUPTION*
at all levels of the church there

The pastors are getting rich and selling access
to their *time* and to their *teaching*
The old and the rich are using their weight
to have *disproportionate control*
of the community
and to get away with
injustice and *debauchery*

Paul says
THIS HAS NO PLACE IN THE KINGDOM OF GOD
It makes no sense in the context of

the **NEW KINGDOM**
where
Wisdom
and
Justice
are the
Currency

And that the purpose of the **CHURCH**
is the
RE-CREATION
of the
WHOLE WORLD
bringing about something
NEW
and
GOOD

II TIMOTHY

The book of **II TIMOTHY** is written by Paul
to his young protégé TIMOTHY

He writes from prison
He's on trial in Rome

He's pretty sure he's **not getting out of this one**

This looks like the **end of Paul's ministry**
and the **end of Paul's life**

and from this place of *seeming defeat*
Paul tells Timothy
not to be

Afraid
or
Ashamed
of his
CALLING

that *leadership is hard*
that *justice is expensive*
that *love is never simple*

BUT THAT IT'S WORTH IT

NEVER BE ASHAMED of the **GOSPEL**
NEVER BE ASHAMED of the **WORK** OF **LOVE** and **JUSTICE**
NEVER BE ASHAMED of the **HARDSHIP** that it BRINGS YOU

This is
a SIGN
that
it's
WORKING

TITUS

The book of **TITUS**
reminds us
that even the Bible
knows that CHURCHES
sometimes
maybe even
frequently
GET IT WRONG

It's about a man named TITUS
who is sent to the island of CRETE
to *restore order* in the churches there

They have **lost their way**
by becoming too much like the CULTURE around them

Their values have become skewed
and the **GOSPEL**
is **obscured** by it

But Paul tells Titus
that it is in **places like this**

where *dishonesty*
and *fraudulent sex*
and *violence*
are the norm

that God is going to make a
New World a Reality
and that the
Preaching
of the
GOSPEL
will be most
clearly presented
through the lives of people

FOLLOWING JESUS
in their community

PHILEMON

The book of **PHILEMON**
can quickly *offend*
our *contemporary sensibilities*

It is written by an early Christian leader
named Paul

and he has **befriended**
a **runaway slave**

And what does he tell the slave to do
He tells him to *go home*

GO BACK TO HIS *SLAVE MASTER*

BUT

To take a **letter** with him
And that is the book that we have today

The letter **tells the slave owner
to WELCOME his slave back**
BUT
NOT AS A SLAVE
AS A BROTHER

Paul understands that

IF

WE WANT THE WORLD TO CHANGE
*WE HAVE TO LIVE
AS IF IT **ALREADY HAS***

HEBREWS

The book of **HEBREWS**
is asking the question
WHAT IS GOD DOING

It looks back at the OLD TESTAMENT
It pulls on stories
all the way back to GENESIS
all through the Hebrew Bible
and reveals that God has been
TELLING A SINGULAR STORY
THROUGH ALL OF IT

A STORY about
GOD ON MISSION
to **BLESS**
ALL THE FAMILIES OF THE EARTH
A GOD WHO WANTS TO
RESTORE
ALL THE COSMOS

A GOD
WHO CARES ABOUT
COMMUNITY and JUSTICE

AND A GOD
WHO HAS ENTERED HUMAN HISTORY
*IN THE PERSON OF **JESUS***

Because the STORY is NOT FINISHED
JESUS
the **HOLY SPIRIT**
and the **CHURCH**
are the
CONTINUATION
of
GOD'S MISSION
in the
WORLD
to
RE-CREATE ALL THINGS

JAMES

The book of **JAMES**
is a *collection of teachings*
from an early church leader named *JAMES*

He deals with questions
about how to **live in community**
he talks
about *lying*
and *slandering*
and *gossiping*
And he talks about **how to take care of the poor**

He talks about how to
SEEK PEACE
and **JUSTICE**
and **COMMUNITY**

But the overarching theme of the whole book
is that

YOUR ACTIONS
ARE YOUR BELIEFS

If you say you
BELIEVE SOMETHING
We know if
It is TRUE
Or NOT
based on
HOW
YOU
LIVE

I PETER

The book of **I PETER**
tells us that when
WE SUFFER
FOR WHAT IS RIGHT
when we
ENDURE PAIN
and ***TRIAL***
and ***STRUGGLE***
for the CAUSES of
GOOD
and **TRUTH**
and **JUSTICE**

We are UNITED WITH the STORY
of EVERYONE
who has sought
a **BETTER WORLD**
and that it is in those moments
of ***TRIAL***
and ***DIFFICULTY***

that we **BUILD UP**
the **VERSION of OURSELVES**
that we
WANT to BE

Our **best version of ourselves**
will always be
FORGED
by who
WE CHOOSE TO BE
WHEN THINGS ARE
HARD

II PETER

The book of **II PETER**
is Peter's last work

He writes the book *knowing*
that it is the *end of his life*
And so he says the book is going to be a
summary of all my teachings
so that they can live on after I am gone

He tells the people
to trust in what they KNOW
to hold to what is GOOD
and what is TRUE

He says to
REMEMBER
In all the things that I have taught you
that the
MOST IMPORTANT THING
is to ***LOVE***

to be concerned about the
WELL BEING OF THOSE AROUND YOU
and that to do so
to ***LIVE A LIFE OF LOVE***
is to be engaged
with the
highest form
of ***TRUTH***
and ***REALITY***

I JOHN

The book of **I JOHN**
is a sermon written
by JOHN the ELDER
to a church in EPHESUS

The church is going through a
season of
confusion
and ***turmoil***
and ***difficulty***

and John says
If you are going to be the kind of people
who can SURVIVE this
You are going to have to

LIVE UP
to the things
YOU SAY YOU BELIEVE

You are going to have to
RETURN
to your
CORE VALUES
and your ***connection*** to this
HIGHER REALITY

John ***reminds*** them that

GOD is ***LIGHT***
GOD is ***TRUTH***
GOD is ***LOVE***

and that those are the things
that can bring us together
SAVE OUR COMMUNITIES
and
make us
WHOLE AGAIN

II JOHN

The book of **II JOHN**
tells us
that there are people out there

who want to DECEIVE us
that want to TRICK us
that want to
LEAD US in the WRONG WAY

And we don't have to *FIND THEM*
They are going to come **LOOKING FOR US**

But the way to ENDURE such troubles
is to **TRUST**
in that which has ALREADY shown itself to be **TRUE**
and to
GROUND OURSELVES
In **LOVE**

III JOHN

The book of **III JOHN**
is a
CORRESPONDENCE
between
two friends
who are both members
of a *COMMUNITY*
that is experiencing
a difficult
season of
tension
and
distrust

The author says that if
we are going to
RECLAIM
what made our
COMMUNITY
great in the first place
If we are going to
SAVE OUR COMMUNITY
It's going to be through
RESPECT
and
TRUST

HOSPITALITY
and
WELCOME

JUDE

The book of **JUDE**
tells us that

Corruption from Leadership Is to be EXPECTED

that we should ANTICIPATE
Corrupt Leaders
and that the *GREED*
of these Leaders
ALWAYS
brings about

SCARCITY

and

CHAOS

but that you can
COMBAT them by

LIVING YOUR LIFE

built on a
FOUNDATION
of
TRUTH

And from there
you can *SEEK*

JUSTICE
and
MERCY

REVELATION

The book of **REVELATION**
is written to a community
of *persecuted churches*
in *modern day TURKEY*

The book is written
to **ENCOURAGE THEM**
to give them **STRENGTH** and **FAITH**
for this circumstance
by one of their pastors
who has been
EXILED
as part of this *persecution*

Things have gotten so *extreme*
that when he goes to write
the only language they can find
the only words that **fit**
are these **POETIC** and **CODED WORDS**

This language that makes it *sound*
like the whole world is being
UNCREATED
like the *demonic armies*
are rising up
to **DESTROY the CHURCH**

And **how will the Church RESIST?**

Will they raise up their own ARMY
Will they FIGHT BACK
Will they raise their SWORDS in VIOLENCE
NO
he writes
They will
OVERCOME
by the
BLOOD of the LAMB
and the
WORD of THEIR TESTIMONY

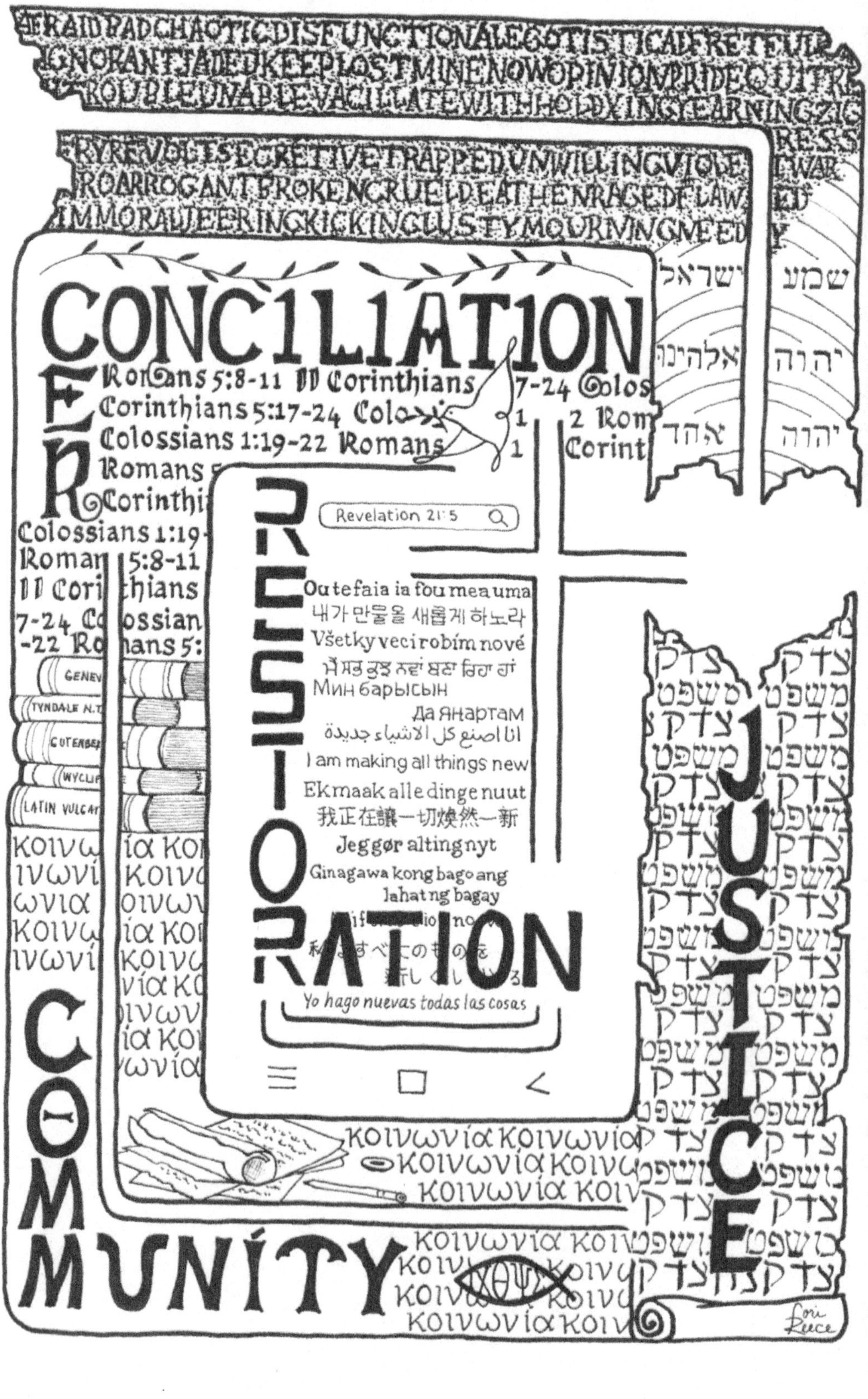

CONCILIATION
Romans 5:8-11 II Corinthians
Corinthians 5:17-24
Colossians 1:19-22 Romans
Revelation 21:5
Ou te faia ia fou mea uma
내가 만물을 새롭게 하노라
Všetky veci robím nové
Мин барысын
Да янартам
انا اصنع كل الاشياء جديدة
I am making all things new
Ek maak alle dinge nuut
我正在讓一切煥然一新
Jeg gør alting nyt
Ginagawa kong bago ang lahat ng bagay
Yo hago nuevas todas las cosas
RATION
JUSTICE
COMMUNITY
GENEVA
TYNDALE N.T.
LATIN VULGATE
שמע ישראל
יהוה אלהינו
יהוה אחד
צדק
משפט
κοινωνία
ΙΧΘΥΣ

by Lori Reece.

For some people, the thought of reading the whole Bible from cover to cover is unimaginable, due to its length. Others may think that reading a book written so long ago would be a waste of time because it couldn't possibly still be relevant or applicable today. This book removes both of those obstacles by distilling each book of the Bible into a single page that connects the reader to a message that still has a bearing on our current world. Even so, there are also people who need a visual to aid them in understanding or remembering the essential message of what they read in the Bible. As an artist, my contribution to this book was to create an image that would help to remove this obstacle too.

    I was asked to design a pen and ink piece that would highlight four themes that are woven into God's story from beginning to end: Justice, Community, Reconciliation and Restoration. These themes are about the importance of relationships, both to God and to each other. The central story of the Bible is that God loves the people He created and He longs to have an ongoing relationship with them. He also expects His people to treat others with the same loving kindness that He extends to us. As I worked on this drawing, I wanted to show how God has stayed on message all the way through thousands of years and multiple writers, so that even today we can read that same message on our devices in many different languages.

    In order to interpret the visual language of my drawing, I would like to guide the reader through the meaning behind my artistic choices. To begin, I chose a rectangular spiral as the basic shape I would follow. This shape usually represents growth, change, or movement along a path. Here God is seen as the source of the action, drawing humanity towards Himself. The spiral starts at the top left and winds inward. The top section shows very chaotic and dark lettering, with many random words depicting human failure and enmity with God. The heart-shaped gap in the path illustrates how our sin separates us from the love of God. Even so, light can be seen shining through the middle of the darkness, indicating God's presence and plan throughout history.

    Long before the Bible was available in written form, God's message to His people was spread by word of mouth in the form of stories, prayers and songs. I chose to represent this period with the words of the Hebrew prayer, the "Shema", which is visible on the top right side above the gap. This prayer was intended to remind God's people that He was to be their one and only God and to draw them to Himself. It says, "Hear O Israel, the Lord is our God. The Lord is one". When God told Moses to begin writing down His promises and His expectations, the language he wrote in was Hebrew. Having recently visited Qumran, where the Dead Sea Scrolls were discovered, I chose the shape of a scroll on which to introduce the first theme, Justice. On the right side of this drawing the word Justice is written in bold letters surrounded by the Hebrew words for justice, "tzedek" and "mishpat".

    Continuing on to the bottom and left corner of the drawing, a transition to the Greek language represents the New Testament writers, with the Greek word "koinonia" flowing through this part. Koinonia means to have communion or fellowship, which is the kind of dynamic relationship that leads to the second theme, community. Several letters written with a reed stylus and ink pot, illustrate the primary method the Apostles used to communicate to the early churches. The "ichthus" fish symbol in this part of the drawing is actually a code that early Christians used to secretly identify other members of their community. The Greek letters inside the fish are an acronym for, "Jesus Christ, God's Son, Savior".

As the spiral moves upwards and then to the right, the advent of printed books is highlighted by the stack of early versions of the Bible. The various New Testament scripture references depicted in this section are about the third theme, Reconciliation. When a relationship is broken, reconciliation can only occur if there is a change in the relationship. God took the initiative to reconcile us to Himself through Christ, while we were still His enemies. He gave us the choice to change our relationship with Him from one of enmity to peace with Him. The olive branches and the dove both symbolize the idea of making peace and repairing relationships. The dove also symbolizes the work of the Holy Spirit, who enables us to restore our relationships with others.

The last theme of the book is Restoration, which in this case means not only to return something to its previous condition. It means to make it new instead, better than it was before. In Revelation 2:5, Jesus says, "I am making all things new". This same statement is repeated in this part of the drawing in 14 different languages. The central rectangular shape in the spiral also resembles a mobile device on which we can now access the Bible globally. At this point in the drawing, the spiral circles around and crosses over itself to form the shape of the cross. It reaches over into the gap on the right to indicate that Jesus is the only way to close that gap between God and man.

God is making us new creatures and bringing His Kingdom into being right now, in the present. His message remains the same. He loves the people He created and He wants to have an ongoing, personal relationship with them. In return, we must carry out His message by creating communities that uphold justice, seek reconciliation, and look for restoration.

Rev.Jeremy Hall, D.Min

I am a husband, a pastor, a writer, a speaker, and a consultant.

I was born and raised in Pensacola, FL. At Samford University in Birmingham, AL I studied religion and church health. During my four years there, I connected with a church plant called Celebration Church, where I served as Associate and Youth Pastor. I have also served on the staff of churches as a youth minister at Christ Our Shepherd Lutheran Church (ELCA) in Peachtree City, Ga and Clairmont Presbyterian Church (PCUSA) in Atlanta, Ga.

Since moving to Atlanta, I've earned my M.Div in Christian Social Ethics and D.Min in Justice and Peacemaking from Mercer University's McAfee School of Theology.

I have partnered with various churches as a growth and general health consultant. I serve as a member of the advisory board for my friends at WORDWALK Inc., as well as speak at youth events, coach other ministers, and lead conversations on youth and family ministry, Christian ethics, Ecclesiastic/Cultural Issues, church planting, and congregational sustainability.

I sense an overwhelming call to preach. I am a gifted listener, and a patient and careful counselor. My creativity is unyielding, and I thrive in diverse and unfamiliar communities. When faced with conflict and transitions in the church, I am resilient and never complacent, but consumed by the work of the Kingdom. I draw on my education in church health to identify goals and barriers towards more vibrant community. In

6 years of ministry I have devoted myself to study, prayer, and research in preparation for everything I have taught, writing tailor-made curricula and sermons. As a leader I am thoughtful, inclusive, and energetic, and in every church I have served, I've been gradually entrusted with more roles and leadership.

Host/Producer of the KINGDOM ETHICS PODCAST and the Virtually Church Podcast.

My passions include:
Preaching, Writing, Congregational Health, Intergenerational Ministry, Theology/Ethics, Biblical Literacy, and Christian Education.

Rev. Jeremy Hall, D.Min.

Revjeremyhall.com

revjeremyhall@gmail.com

@yesimthatjeremy

http://www.linkedin.com/in/jhall2

Lori Reece is an artist who grew up in the tropics of Central America, where she acquired a second language and a taste for exotic fruit. The exuberant beauty of that part of the world also gave her an early sense of wonder, and a keen eye for color and light.

Throughout her many colored days, Lori has been an educator, an entrepreneur, and a caregiver. Besides her paintbrushes, she also holds a Master of Arts in Teaching and has been a doctoral student at the University of Florida.

As an avid reader, Lori has always loved the way that words paint pictures in her mind. In her new book, "This Is How We Know - The Intention of Fruit ", Lori has flipped the script by first speaking in a visual language on nineteen canvases, which are beautifully captured inside the book. Her writing is the act of translating these images back into the language of words, in order to make their meaning clear.

Lori's fruit obsession led to the inspiration for her paintings and the resulting book, as she followed the design pattern of fruit throughout the Bible. She calls the body of work that grew out of this study "visual meditations". Speaking with color and light, Lori takes the reader on a journey that will hopefully create a hunger for discovering who God is, and a desire to be who we were created to be.

Lori lives with her eyes full of wonder, and her heart full of hope on the beautiful Gulf Coast of Florida with her family.

Curious people can find out more about Lori's art at www.lorireece.art.

Mike Rollwagen is a professional communicator with 30 years experience working with others to facilitate their discovery of how their basic world perspectives and decision-making processes have been influenced by the current and historical concepts that are shaping our world. Mike's passion is to engage others in a discovery of intelligible methods that enrich their personal journey through a respectful understanding of philosophical diversity.

WordWalk is a non-denominational organization that supports Christ-focused ministries around the world and in our local communities. We link people with opportunities and give support as they seek to impact others in Christ-like ways. As we come alongside other kingdom ambassadors, our efforts include the volunteering of our common resources and our individual skills. We coordinate, consult, and execute short-term initiatives, and we give sustained provision for missionaries, church-planters, operatives of education, and humanitarian relief. We are a 501c3 non-profit, structured with an active advisory board.

Wordwalk.us

Acknowledgements

The first and most obvious "thank you" goes to the two brilliant contributors to this book. Lori Reece has been a delight to work with and I have learned much from her work. Mike Rollwagen is one of my mentors and dearest friends, it is not an exaggeration to say that this text would not exist without his influence in my young life. Mike taught me how to think about the Bible and how to Love it. Mike was the first to see the potential for a book to come from the video series and took it upon himself to transcribe the videos into their first written iteration.

Next, I must acknowledge my wonderful family, without their support none of my ministry would be possible. They hold me up, they keep me strong, the keep me focused on what matters.

(I wonder if anyone has written this sentence anywhere yet...)
TIKTOK! I must thank TIKTOK and those who have supported me on that platform. Their interest in my way of teaching the Bible, your encouragement spurred me on from a single one-off video to a 65 video series and now to a book!

I *Acknowledge* that there is not a bibliography for this book. As addressed in the intro, these are based on stream-of-consciousness monologues. But that is not to say that they were not researched. While no content was intentionally lifted from another source, before recording a video I would take some time to read the intros to the book from the *New King James Bible, The Common English Bible,* and *The New Interpreters* and

Oxford study versions of the *New Revised Standard Bible*. I would also consult the intros in the *Interpretation, New Interpreters, The People's,* and *The Women's* Bible Commentaries. I also routinely consulted with the transcripts from *The Bible Project* and podcast episodes from *The Bible for Normal People.* For various videos/chapters I consulted other sources both academic and popular.

Thank you to Ben Garrett who helped me workshop the name.

Thank you to my talented editor Sara Little who made the pre-body sections of this book enjoyable … or at least readable.

Made in the USA
Middletown, DE
22 March 2023